P9-ASM-147

THE *Marriage* DICTIONARY

THE UNOFFICIAL, TRUE MEANING OF "I Do"

TOM CAREY

sourcebooks

Published by Sourcebooks, Inc.

P.O. Box 4410, Naperville, Illinois 60567–4410
(630) 961–3900
Fax: (630) 961–2168
www.sourcebooks.com

Printed and bound in the United States of America.
VP 10 9 8 7 6 5 4 3 2 1

To keep your marriage brimming,
with love in the loving cup,
whenever you're wrong, admit it;
whenever you're right, shut up.

—Ogden Nash

For Kathy, who said yes.

abs

1. Rippling six-pack muscles painted on a souvenir T-shirt your wife jokingly buys you on your honeymoon.
2. Rippling six-pack muscles that actually appear on your husband during your honeymoon after a bout of "turista" causes him to lose twenty pounds in three days.

abstinence

What your bride-to-be will want to practice during the three months prior to your wedding, even though the two of you have been living together for two years, "because it'll be so romantic on our wedding night."

ACL

1. Ligament your maid of honor will tear in a desperate dive to retrieve the bouquet.
2. Same ligament your best man will injure while scrambling away from the garter toss.

Adobe Photoshop

Photo retouching software at which you will become an expert after receiving your wedding photos and discovering that, in addition to the embarrassing complexion issues, you spent thirty minutes rocking out on the dance floor with your dress tucked into your pantyhose after a quick trip to the ladies' room.

alfresco

1. The kind of lunch your wife wants to have on your honeymoon.
2. The kind of sex your husband wants to have on your honeymoon.

alterations

1. What your bride's gown will need the day before the wedding, when it is discovered that she has lost eighteen pounds and two dress sizes due to the month-long pre-wedding diet of saltines and Diet Coke she went on so she'd look good in the wedding photos.
2. What you will make in the guest list when it is discovered that your cousin Jim Bob's "plus one" includes his wife, her sister, their aunt, her boyfriend, his three kids and their various pets.

American Embassy

The place you'll be spending most of your time while on the remote, little, out-of-the-way, godforsaken tropical island where your travel agent sends you on your honeymoon. (See also *military coup.*)

amnesia

Unusual medical condition that often afflicts husbands the day after a night out drinking and carousing with "the boys."

anorexic

The apparent condition of the old girlfriend whose photos and love letters your husband insists on keeping in a shoe box on the top shelf of his closet. (See also *busty.*)

arguing

What you are doing whenever you have a disagreement with your spouse, which will last the entire length of your marriage, interspersed with short periods of making up. (See also *discussing.*)

Arthur Murray

Dance academy where you dragged your reluctant fiancé for sixteen weeks to learn how to channel your inner Astaire and Rogers. (See also *waltz* and *graceful*.)

athlete

What your husband still sees when he looks in the mirror.

athlete's foot

The only part of your husband that is still truly athletic.

baby

1. Exclamation following exceptionally passionate sex. (Ex. "Baby, baby, baby!")
2. Exclamation following positive home pregnancy test. (Ex. "Baby, baby, baby?!")

bachelor

Any single male friend who has a discernible heartbeat, walks upright, and is between the ages of twenty and eighty, whom your wife will insist on trying to "fix up" with her single friends.

bachelor party

All-male bash held the week before the wedding, in which the groom and all his friends celebrate the many joys of being a single man, including drinking until they pass out, gambling away their paychecks, and watching an aging stripper with very large breasts gyrate lasciviously while her boom box plays Sir Mix-A-Lot's "Baby Got Back." (See also *guilty*.)

B

bachelorette party

All-female bash held the week before the wedding, in which the bride and all her friends celebrate the many joys of being a single woman, including: drinking until they pass out, talking trash about all the women they know who are not present, and stuffing dollar bills into the G-string of a male erotic dancer with the abdominal muscles of an Olympic gymnast. (See also *innocent.*)

backseat

1. Where you used to go to sneak away from your boyfriend's parents to "make out."
2. Where you will now have to sit when your husband's mother is in the car.

ballet

Dance performed to classical music in an elegant theater before tearful, enraptured wives accompanied by bored, distracted husbands who insist on repeating, "He's gay, y'know," and "Relax, that's a codpiece!" each time the lead male dancer receives applause from the audience.

bathrobe

One of four Christmas gifts you will be receiving from your husband every single year, now that you are married. (See also *nightgown*, *perfume*, and *slippers*.)

beer

Carbonated, malt-based beverage, which, when drunk in quantity, will keep your husband chubby, out of shape, dull-witted, gassy, and sexually unappealing.

beer commercial

Television advertisement for carbonated, malt-based beverage, shown at breaks in professional sporting events meant to convince men like your husband that beer, when drunk in quantity, will make them slim, athletic, witty, and sexually irresistible.

best man

Best friend of the groom, whose wedding responsibilities include: a) organizing the bachelor party, b) making sure the groom is not too hungover from that party to get through a church ceremony without passing out, and c) repeatedly reminding the groom that, "It's still not too late to get out of this."

bikini

1. Bathing suit that reveals every flaw, rogue hair, and bit of flab on your body.
2. Small atoll in the middle of the Pacific Ocean, thousands of miles from anywhere and anyone, which is why it's the only place you'd ever consider wearing one.

bikini line

Portion of your wife's anatomy that advances and retreats, signifying the passing of the seasons as accurately as does the coat of the woolly bear caterpillar.

bimbo

Any woman to whom, while in the company of your wife, you pay a compliment. (Ex. You: "Bill's new wife seems nice, doesn't she?" Your wife: "That bimbo?")

blended

1. What your family will be once your new spouse and her two teenage daughters move into your four-bedroom house with you and your three teenage boys. (See also *Brady Bunch theme song*.)
2. The kind of margaritas you and your spouse will consume each night on the patio after several hours of dealing with all those teenagers.

blue

1. Color of the condom you receive as a gag gift at your bridal shower.
2. Color of your face when said condom fails.
3. Color of the chemically treated swab in your home pregnancy test kit.
4. Color your husband will be painting the den… er, nursery.

bouquet

A flower arrangement carried by the bride, who, during the bouquet-tossing ceremony, will throw it as hard as she can directly to her best friend, who longs to become engaged to her long-time, cold-footed beau. (See also *garter*.)

bowl games

Excuse for your husband to ignore you from approximately December 1 through January 31 every year.

boy–girl

1. Seating arrangement of married couples that allows harmless, spouse-supervised flirting at dinner parties.
2. Name of the website that allows not-so-harmless, unsupervised "flirting" when your spouse is not around.

bra

Decoration draped by your wife over the shower curtain rod in the bathroom. (See *pantyhose.*)

Brady Bunch theme song

What people you meet will inevitably begin singing when you tell them about your prodigious new family situation. (See also *blended.*)

bridal registry

Service provided by department stores that allows you and your spouse to keep track of exactly how much money your friends and relatives are spending on gifts for you.

Brides

Magazine targeting blissfully engaged women, featuring six pages of articles on subjects like choosing a veil or the pros and cons of serving prime rib at the reception, along with over twelve hundred pages of advertising for wedding gowns, china, crystal, tuxedos, caterers, disc jockeys, and orchestras.

bridesmaids

1. A list of friends and relatives you've enlisted as payback for the countless thousands of dollars you've spent over the years on shoes that don't fit, ridiculous hats, bachelorette parties, and atrocious clown-like dresses collecting dust in the back of your closet ever since *their* weddings.

2. Hilarious far-fetched comedy you watch for the first time a few weeks before your wedding, which looks more like a documentary when you watch it again a few weeks after your wedding.

bridesmaid dress

Gown worn by friends and sisters of yours, chosen by you to be so unflattering to them that even if you wake up on your wedding day looking eerily like a cathedral gargoyle, you will surely appear gorgeous in comparison.

busty

The physical appearance of the old girlfriend whose photos and love letters your husband keeps in a shoe box on the top shelf of his closet. (See also *anorexic.*)

cartwheel

What your future brother-in-law will attempt while "dancing" down the aisle to the song "Forever" even though he is fifty pounds heavier than he was in high school when he last attempted one. (See also *tibia*.)

car

Where you'll spend most of the holiday season, now that you have married into a family that includes six aunts, four uncles, twenty-seven nieces and nephews, two grandparents, two step-grandparents, and one great-grandmother...and her girlfriend.

carrot

The kind of cake in which your boyfriend will hide an engagement ring for his surprise proposal at your favorite restaurant. (See also *molar*.)

cat

Animal you would like as a pet, but to which your spouse claims to be allergic. (See also *dog*.)

celibate

What the priest who gives you your pre-marital sexual counseling is.

chair

Something your husband used to hold for you. (See also *coat*, *door*, and *hand*.)

cheap

What your spouse is, when it comes to spending money on anything wedding related. (See also *frugal*.)

China

1. The expensive plates, bowls, saucers, cups, and dishes that you will be receiving from various friends, guests, and relatives at your wedding.
2. Country comprised of 1.3 billion people who couldn't care less about your wedding.

chores

Day-to-day household tasks that you and your spouse supposedly divide equally, but in reality will be done by whoever gets fed up with the filth the quickest.

closet

1. Storage area in your new home that will be divided on an "as needed" basis: 93 percent for you, 7 percent for your husband.
2. What your cousin Blaine from San Francisco will come out of, in front of two hundred fifty startled guests at your wedding reception, after drinking two bottles of champagne and dancing very enthusiastically to "YMCA."

coat

Another thing your husband used to hold for you. (See also *chair*, *door*, and *hand*.)

cocooning

What your husband calls staying at home every night while sprawled out on the couch in his sweatpants and a T-shirt, drinking beer, and zapping through cable TV channels with the remote.

cold

C

1. Illness characterized by the following symptoms in husbands: coughing, sneezing, sore throat, runny nose, whining, need for constant attention, desire for tea and toast with strawberry preserves spread on just the way Mom used to, and which will require three full days off of work and ten days of no chores because, "I have a cold, you know. It could turn into pneumonia!"

2. Relative sexual temperature of wife after waiting on sick husband hand and foot for two weeks.

cologne

One of four Christmas gifts you will be receiving from your wife every single year, now that you're married. (See also *gloves*, *scarf*, and *tie*.)

commitment

What your fiancé was able to offer to his job, his weekly poker game crew, his golf league, his mother, and his favorite fishing TV show, more easily than he was to you.

conversing

What you are doing when you talk about your neighbor's marital difficulties. (See also *gossiping*.)

cotton

Material from which a married woman's underwear is made. (See also *silk*.)

cuddle

Act of warmth and affection that your husband will invariably interpret as foreplay. (See also *kiss*, *hug*, and *snuggle*.)

DJ

Entertainer hired to play recorded music at your wedding reception, who will disregard all requests for your favorite songs, and instead get drunk as a skunk and play "Celebration" by Kool and the Gang (even though you expressly forbade this), "Mony Mony," (the Billy Idol version with the dirty, sing-along lyrics), and "Shout," from the movie *Animal House*, during which he will yell, "Gator!" and then throw himself on the floor in an attempt to look under the bridesmaids' dresses.

dance

The action of moving rhythmically to music with a partner, a skill that most females naturally possess, but that a male acquires only for the short time in his young adulthood when he wishes to meet and impress young women, and abandons thereafter due to mysterious and recurring "knee injuries."

date

Social engagement between two people who are trying to decide whether or not it would be a good idea to have sex.

deposit

What you will not be getting back from the banquet hall due to the damaged chairs, the stained table-cloths and, well, any and all surfaces that could possibly have been damaged by a group of "humans." (See also *x's and o's*.)

discussing

What your spouse is doing whenever she has a disagreement with you. (See also *arguing*.)

dog

Animal you would like as a pet, but to which your spouse claims to be allergic. (See also *cat*.)

door

Yet another thing your husband used to hold for you. (See also *chair*, *coat*, and *hand*.)

doubles

1. Tennis game played by athletic couples who wish to burn a few calories while arguing in public.
2. Size of the drinks said couples order after the game.

driveway

Where your husband will sit, in his idling vehicle, honking the horn and yelling, while you try to get ready to go out.

dysfunctional

State of your relationship according to your wife, who screams at you like a crazy person every couple of weeks, for no apparent reason, when all you're trying to do is sit on your nice new white couch, watch a ballgame, and eat some Cheetos. (See also *relationship*.)

E. coli

The virulent bacteria that will be transferred from your caterers' hygiene-challenged helper to the crème brûlée and subsequently to two-thirds of your guests, who will have fond memories of the bathrooms at your reception hall, though not so many of the reception itself.

early

1. What your husband insists on being everywhere you go together. ("The invitation says 7:30!")
2. What he is in bed, too.

elope

1. What your parents secretly wish you would do after they volunteer to "help" with the wedding expenses.
2. What you seriously consider doing after a couple of months of your parents' "help."

emerge

What your left breast will do from the top of your strapless wedding gown (directly in front of the videographer) during a spirited rendition of the "Chicken Dance." (See also *YouTube*.)

encore

What your wife will want after sex on your wedding night. (See also *ZZZs*.)

engagement

A period of time designated by two people who have decided to get married, in order for: their parents to argue about seating arrange-ments for the reception, the caterers to go out of business, three of the bridesmaids to get their shoes dyed the wrong color, and the minister to run off to Acapulco with the church organist, who has the wedding sheet music.

engraving

Expensive and elaborate printing process that you will use on your wedding invitations, napkins, and matchbook covers, all of which will have your names spelled wrong.

erotica

Sexually explicit material that your spouse enjoys, but that you find boring.

ESP

1. An abbreviation for extrasensory perception, an ability your wife will expect you to possess so as to be able to anticipate her every mood, whim, and desire.
2. The strong feeling you have that you do not possess this ability.

ex

1. Your wife's previous spouse, whom she will remember as a scummy, rotten, low-down, two-timing loser, before you get married.
2. Your wife's previous spouse, whom she will remember as a loving, tender, hardworking example of everything you are not, after you get married.

exchange

What your wealthy and sensitive aunt and uncle will catch you doing with the very expensive but incredibly ugly lamp they gave you as a wedding gift.

Facebook

Social media website where people share photos, videos, and extravagant lies about how fabulous their lives are, upon which you will post details of your wedding, which, according to you, took place in Acapulco on a cliff overlooking the ocean, was attended by LeBron James, Donald Trump, and Jennifer Lawrence, and where Beyoncé performed.

fat

1. Your wife will ask you if she looks like this every time she tries on a new outfit.
2. The chance that you will ever have sex again if you answer the above question wrong.

feelings

What your husband will discuss with you three times in ten years.

Fifty Shades of Grey

1. Novel about dominant/submissive sex and role playing that your spouse wants to use as inspiration to spice up your love life.
2. What you suggest would be a good name for your spouse's underwear drawer, thereby ending any chance of you enjoying a spiced-up love life.

forehead

One of his two body parts that will grow larger after you marry your husband. (See *stomach*.)

foreplay

1. A prelude to intercourse, which, during the first six months of marriage, will last up to an hour or more and include kissing, stroking, fondling, cuddling, back rubs, hot oil massage, candlelit dinners, long walks along the beach holding hands, and slow dancing to Tony Bennett's "The Way You Look Tonight."
2. A prelude to intercourse that, after the first six months of marriage, will consist of a wink and a smack on the butt.

Forever

1. A popular song that inspired a wedding party to dance down the aisle, creating a cute flash mob video viewed thousands of time on YouTube. This will inspire your "friends" in the wedding party to choreograph a similar 10 minute dance they will then do while entering the church, without warning you, the wedding planner, or the minister, even though they know about your strong aversion to "surprises." (See also *cartwheel*.)
2. The amount of time you will spend not speaking to those flash-mob-loving friends.

freeloader

Friend of your spouse who visits, eats all your food, sleeps on your couch, leaves little hairs stuck on your bath soap, and always stays twice as long as you expect him to. (See also *guest*.)

frugal

What *you* are when it comes to spending money on the wedding. (See also *cheap*.)

fuller

The cut of the blue jeans your husband buys so he can claim he still wears the same pants size he wore in high school.

GPS

What your husband now ignores while driving. (See also *map.*)

garage sale

Event held to sell all the items you bought with your spouse's money (at about 25 cents on the dollar) after your spouse finds out about it and files for divorce. (See also *joint bank account.*)

garter

Item of lingerie you are supposed to remove from your wife's leg during the reception and toss, per her instructions, to her best friend's long-time, cold-footed beau. Her plans will be dashed when said beau is in the bathroom during this ceremony, allowing the garter to be snagged by your annoying twelve-year-old nephew who will pester the best friend for the rest of the reception saying, "Hey, baby, when's the honeymoon?" (See also *bouquet.*)

garter belt

1. Item of lingerie you use to keep your stockings up.
2. Item of lingerie you use to keep your husband's "interest" up.

genes

1. The part of the human chromosome that ensures that you and your spouse will eventually, and inevitably, look, sound, and act just like your parents no matter how hard you try not to.
2. The part of the human chromosome that ensures that your children will eventually, and inevitably, look, sound, and act just like you no matter how hard they try not to.

get a room

1. What your inebriated guests will inevitably yell whenever you and your spouse kiss during the reception. I mean every single time.
2. What you will be unable to do on your wedding night when it is discovered that each of you thought the other was in charge of booking a hotel.

gifts

Cash and presents, whose value is a direct reflection of how much you are liked by your friends and relatives, and how much you spent on them when they got married.

gloves

One of four Christmas gifts that you will be receiving from your wife every single year, now that you're married. (See also *cologne, scarf, and tie.*)

gossiping

What the neighbors are doing when they talk about your marital difficulties. (See also *conversing.*)

graceful

What it turns out your fiancé is after several ballroom dance classes. And sadly, it turns out, you are not. (See also *Arthur Murray.*)

grateful

What you turn out to be when it becomes clear that the tribute band you got stuck with cannot play a waltz, so you won't be shown up on the dance floor by your husband's grace and—it must be said—somewhat flamboyant ballroom dance moves.

G

gravy boat

Item of fine china that you were unaware even existed prior to filling out a gift registry. You are now convinced that you cannot live without one, and possibly two.

greeting card

Small token of your love and affection for your wife, featuring a treacly poem and a gauzy photograph of a young couple holding hands and making goo-goo eyes at one another, that you will be sending to her at frequent intervals throughout your relationship, "Just because I was thinking of you, honey." If you know what's good for you. (See also *Hallmark*.)

grocery list

Lengthy, detailed list of food and household items that your husband will leave on the kitchen table when he goes to the store, returning instead with six cartons of Klondike Bars, a head of iceberg lettuce, a tomato (because he knows how much you like salad), a *Car and Driver* magazine, a box of Ritz crackers, a jar of peanut butter, and a box of day-old (30 percent off!) doughnuts.

groom

1. Member of the wedding party whose only duties are to show up on time, at the correct church, and remain somewhat sober until the ceremony ends.
2. Member of the wedding party most likely to forget one or more of his duties.

guest

Any friend of yours who visits and eats all your food, sleeps on your couch, leaves little hairs stuck on your bath soap, and always stays twice as long as you expect him to. (See also *freeloader*.)

guilty

The way your husband will act when you ask him what, *exactly*, went on at his bachelor party. (See also *lie*.)

hair

What will begin disappearing from your husband's head as soon as you exchange wedding vows, and then begin appearing shortly thereafter in his nose and ears.

hairy

1. Husband's razor, after you use it to shave your legs.
2. Fight that occurs after your husband attempts to use his razor after you do and loses a quart of blood down the bathroom sink.

Hallmark

Company you should buy stock in. (See also *greeting card*.)

hand

Still another thing your husband used to hold for you. (See also *chair*, *coat*, and *door*.)

handkerchief

The one crucial item you will forget to have with you for your walk down the aisle even though you know you're a crier. (See also *sleeve*.)

hasty

The kind of wedding you will plan after you find out you're knocked up and you will be left out of your Great Aunt Prudence's will if that baby shows up three months after the ceremony. (See also *home pregnancy test*.)

hell

Where your spouse will be going according to your very Catholic great aunt. (See also *purgatory* and *limbo*.)

Here Comes the Bride

1. Song played by church organist as you walk down the aisle at the start of your wedding ceremony.
2. Phrase your husband will utter jokingly during a crucial moment of wedding-night lovemaking that will cause you to lose your concentration… and your temper.

history

1. Details of your sexual past, which you reveal to your fiancée in an emotional spate of truth-telling during your pre-wedding counseling session.
2. Your engagement after your fiancée learns those details.

home

What a house is during a marriage. (See also *house.*)

home pregnancy test

Product you purchased at a pharmacy forty-five-minutes from your house to make sure your Great Aunt Prudence, who lives in your little town and is a very wealthy busybody, will not find out that you're having sex before marriage. (See also *hasty.*)

honey

Term of endearment used by newlyweds which ironically also means "bee vomit."

honeymoon

Trip newlyweds take to an exotic, romantic resort to discover passion, closeness, and what their spouse really does in the bathroom.

house

Domicile purchased by married couples so they have someplace to pour all their money. (See also *real estate*.)

hug

Act of warmth and affection that your husband will inevitably interpret as foreplay. (See also *cuddle, kiss*, and *snuggle*.)

hunting

Male-bonding ritual that your husband and several of his pals use as an excuse to drive off-road vehicles through the mud, fire large noisy weapons, go to the bathroom outdoors, and mercilessly slaughter God's warm, fuzzy, defenseless little creatures.

ice pack

Plastic pouch filled with ice, commonly used to reduce swelling in head injuries. (See also *idiot*.)

idiot

Word you use during the wedding reception to describe your wife's 6-foot, 4-inch, 230-pound, very short-tempered brother, unaware that he is standing directly behind you at the time. (See also *ice pack*.)

I'll let you know

Wifespeak for "no."

imaginative

Any idea you come up with to spice up your sex life, but that your spouse finds too gross. (See also *kinky*.)

impotence

Physical manifestation of a husband's lack of sexual desire brought on most often by stress, alcohol consumption, or by the sight of his wife wearing her flannel nightgown to bed again.

inch

A unit of measure, the actual length of which is consistently exaggerated by men.

incontinence

Condition that your spouse's great-aunt Sylvia suffers from. Many guests at your wedding reception will be introduced to said condition when she is mistakenly seated at the table farthest away from the bathrooms. (See also *seating arrangement*.)

ingrown

What several of your wife's toenails will become after ten hours of having her feet crammed into a pair of shoes that are at least two sizes too small, but that she insisted on wearing because they were the only ones that really looked good with her wedding dress.

in-law

Person from your spouse's side of the family whom you have never met before, but who will show up a week before the wedding, sleep on your living room couch, spend hours in your only bathroom, and eat all your Double Stuf Oreos. This person will give you a pair of cow-shaped ceramic "Welcome to Wisconsin" salt and pepper shakers as a wedding gift.

innocent

The way your wife will act when you question her about what, exactly, went on at her bachelorette party. (See also *guilty*.)

insomnia

Condition your husband will insist you must be suffering from when you can't sleep due to his endless snoring, thrashing, babbling, and teeth grinding.

intestinal

The type of illness a third of your wedding guests will develop after enjoying the lovely seafood buffet that the caterer thoughtfully set up near the heat register.

invitations

The cards you sent to request the presence (and presents) of 350 of your closest friends, relatives, and coworkers, only to find forty of them—the ones he promised to mail six weeks ago—in your fiancé's coat pocket three days before the event. (See also *involuntary manslaughter*.)

involuntary manslaughter

The charge you can probably plead to after you allegedly kill him. (See also *invitations*.)

Jabba the Hutt

Movie character who bears a remarkable resemblance to your mother-in-law, which you point out after several cocktails, at your rehearsal dinner, nearly causing the wedding to be called off.

jack

1. Indispensable tire-changing tool, the lack of which will leave you and most of the wedding party stranded on the median of the expressway when the limo blows a tire on the way from the church to the reception.
2. What you, your spouse, and apparently the driver know about changing a tire.

Jack in the Box

Fast food restaurant where you will end up on your wedding night having forgotten to eat for over 10 hours.

Jacques Cousteau

What the paramedics will call you behind your back after they are called to your honeymoon suite to revive you after some erotic underwater wedding night Jacuzzi lovemaking goes awry. (See also *Jacuzzi* and *mouth-to-mouth*.)

Jacuzzi

Whirlpool tub in the honeymoon suite in which you will attempt some questionable but erotic wedding night moves. (See also *mouth-to-mouth*.)

Jell-O

One of only two foods your husband has ever actually learned to "cook." (See also *macaroni and cheese*.)

jelly jar

Glass container adorned with pictures of the Scooby-Doo gang that your husband will insist on using as a drinking glass, despite the hundreds of dollars' worth of elegant glassware you carefully registered for.

Jenny Craig

Weight loss pioneer whose diet program you will pay hundreds of dollars to join in order to look good on your wedding day, and whom you will frequently refer to as "that bitch" due to the extreme mood swings that will occur during your starvation-level calorie-restricted regimen.

Jesus Just Left Chicago

Awesome blues rock song that the ZZ Top tribute band—a last-minute replacement for the fifteen-piece string orchestra that was scheduled to play at your reception but canceled at the last minute—will play seven times in three hours to the sheer delight of your ultra-religious family members. (See also *ZZ Top.*)

jewelry appraiser

Professional gemstone expert to whom your fiancée will take her engagement ring hours after you propose. This will enable her to insure it for its proper value so it will be safe, and also ensure that you spent the recommended two months' salary, so *you* will be safe. (See also *two months' salary.*)

joint bank account

Checking account that allows you to spend your spouse's money any way you want. (See also *garage sale.*)

kayak

Notoriously unstable boat that your spouse will insist on renting during your honeymoon, even though he knows you can't swim. (See also *salt water*.)

keg

1. Container for beer that your fiancé will have at his bachelor party.
2. Container for beer that your new husband's body will begin to resemble after marriage due to excessive consumption of that beverage.

keeper

1. What your husband's very drunk uncle will loudly and continually proclaim after his third double scotch, as in, "Yep, she's a keeper all right!"

2. What your best man promised to be for your uncle ("Don't worry, I'll be his keeper.") before he found out that said uncle had a very pretty and "available" daughter, with whom he will spend most of the evening in the back seat of that uncle's car. (See also *underage.*)

Keeping Up with the Kardashians

The kind quality programming you will find your husband watching on his "state of the art" flat screen TV in his man cave. (See also *plasma.*)

kids

Result of spontaneous, exciting, passionate sex, whose arrival will prevent you from having spontaneous, exciting, passionate sex ever again.

kilt

What your Scottish father in-law will wear to your wedding. (See also *nothing.*)

kinky

Any idea your spouse comes up with to enliven sex that you think is gross. (See also *imaginative*.)

kiss

Act of warmth and affection that your husband will inevitably interpret as foreplay. (See also *cuddle*, *hug*, and *snuggle*.)

kitchen

Place where everyone will gather during your post-wedding, pre-reception party, even though you spent three days cleaning every room in the house but that one.

labor

What your eight-and-a-half-months-pregnant sister and maid of honor will go into about three quarters of the way down the aisle during your wedding procession.

lace

Fabric used in certain bra styles worn by your wife while you are dating. (See also *sports*.)

last name

What your husband will want you to change, even though you have built a successful career and reputation in the business world, and despite the fact that your maiden name is Smith and his is Wizenjankowskowitz.

late

1. What your wife will inevitably be when you're in a hurry to get to a party.
2. What her period will be a few weeks after that party where you both had a few too many drinks, forgot to go to the drugstore, and figured, "Oh, what the hell. Just this once won't make any difference."

lie

What your husband will do when you ask him what, exactly, went on at his bachelor party (See also *guilty*.)

limbo

1. Song and dance that the DJ will use to get your guests "participating." Which will result in your sexy-mini-dress-wearing niece displaying her panties for all to see, *AND* in your new father-in-law's back making an eerie crackling sound as they tried to find out the answer to the age-old question "how low can you go?" (See also *traction* and *zebra*.)
2. Where any children that you and your fiancé have will end up if you don't hurry up, get married, and get them baptized, according to your very Catholic great aunt. (See also *purgatory* and *hell*.)

limerick

Risqué five-line poem your father will recite for your Evangelical Christian mother-in-law at the rehearsal dinner. (See also *Nantucket*.)

lingerie

Ill-fitting, unflattering, and downright strange-looking underwear you will receive from your husband on your birthday after he DVR-ed and watched the Victoria's Secret Fashion Show one too many times.

lukewarm

1. Temperature of the champagne served by the clueless caterer at your reception.
2. The reaction of your in-laws to the news that you'll be moving in with them for a while after you marry, "Just until we get on our feet."

macaroni and cheese

One of only two foods your husband has ever actually learned to "cook." (See also *Jell-O*.)

maid of honor

Bride's closest and dearest friend, whom the groom will meet for the first time at the rehearsal dinner, and either fall madly in love with, thereby delaying the wedding plans, or hate intensely, thereby delaying the wedding plans.

manorexic

What your husband will become after seeing the movie *Magic Mike* and finding out you are having your bachelorette party at a "ladies only" strip club. (See also *abs.*)

manscaping

Procedure your husband will try to do himself at home before the honeymoon, using wax to peel off his thick and somewhat unsightly chest hair. (See also *nipples.*)

map

Chart that your husband used to ignore while driving. (See also *GPS*.)

marriage

Sacred relationship between a man and a woman, in which they promise to love, honor, and cherish one another, even after their body parts begin to wrinkle, sag, and cease to function properly.

marriage counselor

Thrice-divorced professional therapist who will help you and your spouse communicate more effectively, discuss disagreements in a fair and rational manner, and divide the responsibilities of your marriage so that you will be able to celebrate your love for one another and strengthen your love partnership. At least long enough for her to make a couple more payments on the Beemer.

maybe

Wifespeak for "no."

military coup

Violent government overthrow that will occur on the remote, little Caribbean island where your travel agent sends you on your honeymoon. (See also *American Embassy.*)

minister

Clergyman who will perform your wedding ceremony, even though you and your spouse haven't been to church in years, have been shacked up together for months, and are only doing the "church thing" for a few elderly and easily shocked relatives. (See also *sermon.*)

molar

The tooth you will break after an oblivious waiter brings out the slice of carrot cake where your engagement ring is hidden *while* your boyfriend is in the bathroom, working up the courage to propose. (See also *carrot* and *tip.*)

mold

1. What you will desperately attempt to do to your husband's manners, hygienic practices, and housekeeping habits.
2. What will grow on your husband's shower curtain when you fail in this attempt and finally get separate bathrooms.

money

Medium of financial exchange that a newly married couple rarely has, and yet still seems to be able to fight about.

monsoon

Season that coincides with your honeymoon on the remote, little, out-of-the-way, godforsaken tropical island where your travel agent sends you on your honeymoon.

mother

Your female parent, who *is* an expert in homemaking, cooking, childcare, entertaining, real estate, health care, fashion, and travel.

mother-in-law

Your spouse's female parent, who *thinks* she's an expert on homemaking, cooking, childcare, entertaining, real estate, health care, fashion, and travel.

mouth-to-mouth

The kind of resuscitation your husband will require after attempting some unfortunate erotic positions in the honeymoon suite Jacuzzi. (See also *Jacques Cousteau*.)

Nantucket

Small resort town on Cape Cod in Massachusetts where the man in your father's favorite poem is from. (See also *limerick*.)

nap

What your grandfather, who has a deviated septum and snores like a freight train, will take in the front pew of the church in the middle of your wedding ceremony.

neighbors

People who live near you and who are never home when you need to borrow jumper cables or power tools, but who magically appear in their backyard whenever you and your spouse are having a particularly juicy argument. (See also *gossiping*.)

nest egg

The money you were saving for retirement, which your spouse will invest with a friend of a friend who knows a guy whose cousin has a "can't miss" stock tip. (See also *zip*.)

newlyweds

What you and your spouse will officially be considered until the date of your first anniversary or until you go a week without having sex, whichever comes first.

nightgown

One of four Christmas gifts you will be receiving from your husband every single year, now that you are married. (See also *bathrobe*, *perfume*, and *slippers*.)

nipples

What your husband will inadvertently and painfully remove when he uses a do-it-yourself hair removal product at home, necessitating a very embarrassing trip to the emergency room and some highly unusual plastic surgery. (See also *manscaping*.)

no-shows

What twelve people who sent you RSVPs for your reception will be, costing you $650 in uneaten soup, salad, twice-baked potato, and Chicken Kiev.

nothing

1. What your Scottish father-in law will be wearing underneath his kilt. (See *kilt.*)
2. What your wife says she wants for her birthday, after she booked a trip to the South of France "on a whim" as her actual gift, when in fact she expects you to get her something. (See also *ESP.*)

Notre Dame

1. Historic Catholic cathedral in Paris considered by many to be one of the most beautiful examples of French Gothic architecture, and which you hope to someday visit.
2. University in South Bend, Indiana, whose football team will be playing an important game on the afternoon of your wedding, leading all the men in the wedding party to spend the entire reception gathered around a TV in the bar next door to the venue. The only Notre Dame your husband is on board with visiting.

numb

What your face will feel like after an entire day of fake smiling for wedding pictures, introductions to people whose names you can't recall, and wedding night sex.

obey

The word in traditional wedding vows that follows "to love, honor, and…" and that will cause your beautiful, blushing bride to snort derisively and remark, "When pigs fly, Romeo," loudly enough for the minister, the videographer, and many of the shoppers at the mall next door to hear.

oboe

1. Woodwind instrument known for its beautiful sound and for its high level of complexity.
2. Instrument that your spouse's aunt will insist her young son, Otto, play at your wedding.

Ode to Joy

1. Musical piece composed by Beethoven known for its beautiful sound and for its high level of complexity.
2. Piece young Otto will choose to "play" at your wedding.

off-white

The color of the dress your mother-in-law helpfully suggests you ought to be wearing at your wedding.

oh

What your husband replies when you say, "I love you," to him while he's watching a play-off game on TV.

oh oh

What your husband says, during the commercial break, when he gets up to go to the bathroom and finds that you have stuffed all his ties down the toilet.

okra

The only vegetable your caterer will be able to find on short notice after a power outage knocks out his refrigerators, spoiling 90 percent of the food he had originally planned to serve at your reception.

optical illusion

What your wife will insist you saw at the reception when you could have sworn that she was passionately kissing the very handsome lead singer of the band during their smoking rendition of Maroon Five's "Sugar."

orange

The tint of your skin after you burn, then peel, then use the phony tan makeup that you bought in the airport drugstore after your honeymoon on the remote, little, out-of-the-way, godforsaken tropical island where your travel agent sent you for your honeymoon.

orphan

What you'll wish you were when you see the outfit your mother plans to wear to your wedding.

orthodontia

1. What your poor parents had to pay for because as a teenager you looked as though you could eat an apple through a picket fence.
2. What you'll need to begin saving for now, if you plan to have kids who will inevitably inherit your original good looks. (See also *genes*.)

pantyhose

Decoration draped over the shower curtain rod in the bathroom. (See *bra*.)

paper

What most of your meals come wrapped in, now that you're married and are both working ten hours a day.

penis

The part of the male anatomy where the brain is located.

perfume

One of four Christmas gifts you will be receiving from your husband every single year, now that you are married. (See also *bathrobe*, *nightgown*, and *slippers*.)

perhaps

Wifespeak for "no."

personality disorders

Any of the truly maddening habits (such as fingernail biting, door slamming, and drinking milk straight out of the carton) that your spouse has, all of which certainly indicate a need for psychological help. (See also *quirks*.)

pink

Color of your husband's boxer-briefs after he washes them with your red sweatshirt.

pizza

What a husband means when he says, "Don't worry, honey, it's my night to fix dinner."

plasma

1. The kind of flat screen TV your husband will insist on purchasing because of its "state-of-the-art" picture quality. (See also *Keeping Up with the Kardashians*.)
2. What you and your husband will have to donate twice a week for the next 10 years to pay for that TV.

poker

1. Card game played once a month by your husband and his buddies, during which they smoke fat, smelly cigars, gamble too much money, drink too much beer, and stay out way too late.
2. Kind of face put on by your husband (and Lady Gaga) when he denies that he "drank too much, gambled too much, and stayed out way too late."
3. Fireplace implement you swing at him after he tells you all those lies.

prenuptial agreement

Legal document signed by a husband and wife, in which they agree on the equitable distribution of assets in the event of a divorce, but which neglects important marital issues, like who gets to use the bathroom first in the morning.

purgatory

Your eternal destination, according to your very Catholic great aunt. (See also *limbo* and *hell.*)

quack

The doctor who told your eight-weeks-pregnant wife that her abdominal discomfort and nausea was "just a little heartburn."

quadraphonic

The kind of stereo that was popular in the 90s and is your fiancé's prized possession, which he insists on keeping when you move in together.

quaint

Online description for the drafty, roach-infested bed-and-breakfast where you and your spouse spent a long anticipated anniversary romantic weekend, while getting to know the owner, Ray Bob; his wife (and cousin) Jimmie Sue; their ten kids; and various barnyard animals.

Quaker

Religion of your spouse's cousin, which causes you to make a joke about oatmeal upon your introduction and every time when his name comes up. (See also *sense of humor.*)

qualified

The kind of "yes" you got the first time you proposed.

quality

The kind of sex you want. (See *quantity.*)

quantity

The kind of sex your spouse wants. (See *quality.*)

question

What you dreamed your fiancé would pop sometime before the last of your three kids graduates from middle school.

quickie

What the best man and your spouse's sister, both of whom are married, will attempt to have in the men's room of the reception hall, unaware that the wireless microphone he used to give his toast is still in his possession and very much working. (See also *quiet.*)

quiet

What the best man and your spouse's sister definitely are not. (See also *quickie*.)

quinine

1. Kind of mixer the bartender at your wedding will have on hand.
2. What you will be prescribed when you return from your honeymoon. As a result of your run in with Malaria.

quirks

Any of the totally harmless, adorable little habits you have (like fingernail biting, door slamming, and drinking milk straight from the carton) that seem to drive your spouse crazy. (See also *personality disorders*.)

quiver

1. What your wife used to do in delighted anticipation of whatever new and exciting sexual fantasy you came up with.
2. What your spouse does now in revulsion at the thought of whatever new and exciting sexual fantasy you're going to come up with next.

RSVP card

Monogrammed notecard with attached postage sent out with wedding invitation that may or may not be returned to the bride at any time prior to the wedding, even in the church vestibule five minutes before the ceremony. These cards indicate a desire and intention to attend the wedding and may be amended to include extra guests, children, and pets.

real estate

What your house is called during divorce proceedings. (See also *home.*)

re-gifting

1. Practice of "recycling" gifts you receive but despise so much that you don't even want to spend time and energy returning them.
2. Practice that you will partake in now that you've received dozens of gifts that you despise.
3. Practice you will get caught partaking in when your boss opens a box containing an ornate tea set at her anniversary party that she originally gave to you as a wedding gift. A potentially embarrassing and job-threatening gaffe, except for the fact that the tea set was originally a re-gift.

rehearsal

Get-together held the night before the wedding during which the bride and groom will learn where they'll stand at the church during the ceremony.

rehearsal dinner

Get-together held the night before the wedding during which the bride and groom will learn where they'll stand with their in-laws after the ceremony.

relationship

Personal arrangement between you and your husband, wherein he agrees to sit like a lump on the couch, silently zapping from channel to channel searching for some TV show (which apparently has yet to be developed because he never stops at one long enough to see what it's about, unless there's a naked woman on, in which case he turns the sound way down so as to try to fool you into thinking that he's not watching soft porn), and wherein you agree to do all the chores, remember all his family members' birthdays, and periodically remind him of the benefits of personal hygiene. (See also *dysfunctional*.)

religion

Organization of people who share a set of deeply held, sacred, and spiritual beliefs and customs. All of which you'll have to pretend to adopt for several weeks if you want to get married in a really cool church.

remote

1. The only household appliance, besides the refrigerator, that your husband is capable of operating properly.
2. The chance you will get to see more than two minutes of any TV show if your husband is in charge of finding "something good" to watch.

restaurant

Public eating establishment that will be at its most crowded the night you present your girlfriend with a "surprise" diamond ring, which she will turn down, loudly and firmly, before walking out in front of the maître d', the strolling violinist, the waitresses, the girl who sells roses, the busboys, and dozens of your fellow diners.

rightside up

The way you (and your mother, and her mother) put glasses in the cupboard. (See also *upside down*.)

ring

1. Item of jewelry couples bestow on one another symbolizing an eternity.
2. High watermark on bathtub that symbolizes that your husband hasn't cleaned it in an eternity.

romance

What will go out of your marriage forever the moment your wife comes into the bathroom and plops down on the toilet while you're brushing your teeth.

salt water

What you will barf up after your spouse tips over your kayak and has to drag you to the beach to administer CPR on that amazing moonlit excursion you got roped into. (See also *kayak*.)

scarf

One of the four Christmas gifts that you will be receiving from your wife every single year, now that you're married. (See also *cologne, gloves*, and *tie*.)

seating arrangement

Precise layout of the dining area at your reception which will be a source of recurring nightmares for months. No matter how often you reorganize it, it will end up having your uncle with the drinking problem next to the bar, your cousin at the same table with your spouse's brother whom she used to date and now hates, and his new wife with the enormous knockers. Also, your least favorite aunt and uncle will be seated next to your spouse's least favorite aunt and uncle, who will enjoy each other's company so much that they'll plan a return trip to visit you each summer and stay at your place, "Because you've got so gol-dang much room."

secular officiant

Supposedly non-denominational person conducting the wedding ceremony, whom you have reluctantly agreed to use because of your fiancée's parents' strident atheism, to the horror of your deeply religious Southern Baptist family. (See also *Wiccan*.)

sense of humor

Something that your spouse's Quaker cousin does not seem to have when it comes to his religion. (See also *Quaker*.)

sermon

Inspirational, forty-five-minute speech delivered by the minister at your wedding, in which he will be unable to resist the urge to comment on the decline in people's moral fiber, how loosening sexual mores have contributed to the downfall of the church, the government, society in general, and how we're all just "going to Hell in a handcart!" (See also *minister*.)

sex

What couples who are not yet married do in bed. (See also *sleep.*)

shoes

The only product you ever actually purchase from the Victoria's Secret catalog, to the dismay of your husband. (See *Victoria's Secret.*)

shotgun

1. The kind of weapon that your drunk uncle will turn out to have in the trunk of his car, which he will fire wildly at the best man and his young and "innocent" daughter after he finds them partially dressed in the back seat. (See also *underage.*)
2. The kind of wedding that your niece and best man will have 10 weeks later.

silk

Material from which a single woman's underwear is made. (See also *cotton.*)

sink

1. What your hopes will do when you wake up one morning to find yourself staring at the sleepy face of your spouse, and when you realize that

you will be waking up to that face every morning for the rest of your life.

2. Place in the bathroom where your husband collects freshly shaved whiskers.

sleep

What couples who are married do in bed. (See also *sex*.)

sleeve

Part of your $12,000 wedding dress you will be forced to use having forgotten a handkerchief. (See also *handkerchief*.)

slippers

One of four Christmas gifts you will be receiving from your husband every single year, now that you are married. (See also *bathrobe, nightgown*, and *perfume*.)

snuggle

Act of warmth and affection that your husband will inevitably interpret as foreplay. (See also *cuddle, hug*, and *kiss*.)

soap

1. Bar or liquid placed on the edge of a sink by husbands, specifically for washing hands.

2. Tiny scented heart-shaped items placed in a

crystal dish on the edge of sink by wives, spe-cifically NOT meant for washing your hands. (See also *towels*.)

soap opera

1. Television dramas that your wife watches con-stantly, which feature lots of sex, lying, decep-tion, divorce, lawsuits, crime, and all-around despicable behavior.
2. Your in-laws' personal dramas, the details of which your wife listens to constantly, which fea-ture lots of sex, lying, deception, divorce, law-suits, crime, and all-around despicable behavior.

someday

Wifespeak for "never."

soon

Wifespeak for "later."

Spanx

Compression-style undergarment that allows a bride to sport a perfect hourglass figure on her wedding day, but which leaves deep red lines embedded in her skin for up to four weeks.

sports

Style of bra worn by your wife now. (See also *lace.*)

stomach

One of his two body parts that will grow larger after you marry your husband. (See also *forehead.*)

stripper

Chubby, fifty-ish, lavishly stretch-marked "professional entertainer" who will perform at your bachelor party by twirling around in circles and removing her clothing. She will also perform at your brother's bachelor party, your best friend's bachelor party, your best friend's brother's thirtieth birthday party and your boss's retirement bash. Soon you will be on a first-name basis and may even begin exchanging Christmas cards.

stud

1. Piece of lumber used to brace wallboard in home construction, which your husband will buy in large quantity in order to "finish" your basement.
2. What using power tools, getting sawdust all over himself, and wearing a leather tool belt will make him feel like. Which is, of course, the reason he bought the lumber in the first place.

surprise

The kind of party your wife will throw for you at every milestone birthday, even though you have repeatedly begged her not to. It will include insufferable coworkers bearing gag gifts, relatives and in-laws you can't stand, nosy neighbors who are there mostly for the free food, and all your married couple friends who will now expect you to help plan and execute their surprise parties.

sweatpants

One of the items your wife will begin wearing to bed shortly after the wedding. (See also *wool socks* and *X-Large T-Shirt*.)

tan

What you will try desperately to get during the one sunny day of your honeymoon. (See also *third degree.*)

television

An electronic marital aid that will keep you from being bored if you leave it on during sex.

testosterone

Human hormone that causes facial hair growth, muscularity, a deep voice, speeding tickets, a love of golf, NASCAR racing, war, fist fights, fantasy football and the overwhelming desire to purchase cocktails for women with nicknames like "Boom Boom."

third degree

1. The kind of burn you will get while trying desperately to get a tan during the one sunny day of your honeymoon. (See also *tan*.)
2. The kind of questioning you will get when coming home from a "business meeting" at 2 a.m.

tibia

Leg bone your future brother-in-law will snap while attempting a cartwheel in the church aisle. (See also *cartwheel*.)

tie

One of the four Christmas gifts that you will be receiving from your wife every single year, now that you're married. (See *cologne*, *gloves*, and *scarf*.)

tiff

Any disagreement between you and your spouse that does not result in a visit from the police.

'til what do we part?

Your husband's amusing reply to the minister when the traditional vows are read.

tip

What the oblivious waiter who brought out your "engagement ring" cake at the wrong time will not be getting. (See also *molar.*)

toast

1. Touching and emotional moment during the wedding reception when the best man will take the microphone, ask for everyone's attention, and tell a rambling story about all the women in the groom's past who could not quite manage to get him to the altar. This story will include these women's names, current whereabouts, and a detailed physical description of each one, and will be captured on many devices, to be enjoyed for years to come.
2. What your chance of having sex with your new wife will be after she endures the best man's speech.

toilet seat

Part of commode that, despite the laws of physics, develops the ability to defy gravity immediately after you begin sharing a bathroom with your husband.

towels

1. Terry cloth items hung near the sink by husbands for drying hands.
2. Small, monogrammed decorative items hung near the sink by wives, which are NOT meant for drying hands. (See also *soap.*)

traction

1. What your new father-in-law will be in for a week after attempting to "Limbo down" at your reception. (See also *limbo.*)
2. What your husband will be unable to get in his fancy rental dress shoes, resulting in him being in the next hospital bed over from your dad.

trash

The only thing in the house that your husband takes out less often than you.

trivia(l)

Any subject your husband brings up while you're watching one of the 27 *Real Housewives* episodes you are hoarding on your DVR.

tub

1. Place where your thoughtful husband used to prepare a luxurious bath for you, complete with bubble bath, scented candles, and romantic music.
2. Place where your husband now prepares freshly caught fish, complete with bones, guts, and "outdoorsy" aroma.

turkey

1. Traditional Thanksgiving dinner always attended by your spouse's ultra-conservative Uncle Ed, who will rail on at length about how Ronald Reagan sits at the right hand of God and how Franklin D. Roosevelt ruined this great nation.
2. Your spouse's Uncle Ed.

tuxedo

Formal attire for men, designed specifically so that even the most fashion-sense-deprived among them can look good for at least the hour or two it takes to get through the wedding ceremony and picture-taking.

two months' salary

Arbitrary figure designated by jewelry retailers as the amount that you must spend for the tiny bit of metal and polished rock that you give to your fiancée so she won't think you're cheap. (See also *jewelry appraiser.*)

umbrella

Hand-held rain shelter that is available at the front desk of the hotel on the remote, little, out-of-the-way, godforsaken tropical island where your travel agent sends you on your honeymoon, reasonably priced at $250.

uncapped

The way your spouse always leaves the toothpaste tube, which lets the toothpaste harden into a shiny crust around the top of the tube, until the morning you squeeze it so hard in an effort to dispense a usable amount that it bursts free all at once, with enough force to send you crashing into the tub.

underage

Your drunk uncle's daughter, who will spend most of your reception with the best man in the back seat of her daddy's car in the parking lot. (See also *shotgun*.)

underarm

Area of your body that, on your wedding day, will perspire at a rate so unprecedented and spectacular that your gown will be saturated all day despite deodorant, talcum powder, and dress shields.

underexposed

The condition of every single roll of film shot at your wedding.

underwear

What the sexy videographer's assistant at your wedding reception is clearly *not* wearing. (See also *yoga pants*.)

unpack

What the customs inspector on the remote, little, out-of-the-way, godforsaken tropical island where your travel agent sends you on your honeymoon will make you do, even though you're late for your flight, there's not another flight until tomorrow, and there are thirty other people in line who look like extras from an episode of *Breaking Bad*.

U

upside down

The way your spouse puts glasses in the cupboard. (See also *rightside up*.)

usher

1. Wedding ceremony job given to any male friend whom you don't quite like enough to actually include in the wedding party.
2. Name of singer whose "amazing" washboard abs your wife comments on every chance she gets while giving your beer belly a look of disdain.

vacuum

1. Electrical household appliance whose operation will remain a complete mystery to your husband even though he is able to disassemble and reassemble a computer blindfolded.
2. State of your husband's brain during football season.

viaduct

Posh location where the guy from whom your fiancé bought your ring operates out of a 1989 Ford Econoline van. (See also *zirconium*.)

Victoria's Secret

1. Catalog your husband reads in the bathroom since you made him cancel his subscription to *Playboy*.
2. Label on package left by UPS on your doorstep that will cause your husband to be extremely excited. Until he finds out it contains shoes. Who knew they sold shoes?

virgin

1. Beautiful, safe, U.S.-governed islands in the Caribbean Sea, where couples who are not clients of your travel agent frequently honeymoon.

2. What your wife will want to act like on your wedding night, even if she's had more pairs of shoes under her bed than Amy Schumer.

vision

1. What you will be in your $4500 lace and satin wedding gown.
2. What you will have on your wedding night after too many choco-tinis.

vote

What you and your spouse dutifully cast each election year, even though you disagree about virtually everything political and you always cancel one another out anyway.

V

vow

1. Promise you make while kneeling before the altar on your wedding day to love, honor, and cherish your spouse for the rest of your life.
2. Promise you make while kneeling before the toilet on your wedding night never to drink two quarts of warm champagne, five glasses of wine, and twelve beers again for the rest of your life.

wallpaper

Decorative wall covering in your condo that was acceptable to your wife for the three years you lived together there, but that she cannot bear to look at a second longer, now that you are married.

waltz

Song in a ¾ time signature traditionally played at weddings so you can show off the moves you learned in the ballroom dance classes you attended for sixteen weeks. Unfortunately, a very different tempo from "Jesus Just Left Chicago." (See also *Arthur Murray*.)

waxing

Procedure used to remove hair from upper lip that will tear a two-inch hunk of skin out of your face two days before your wedding.

we'll see

Wifespeak for "no."

white

Color your husband's boxers must have been at one time.

white guy overbite

1. Intense, lip-biting facial expression on the faces of all your straight male guests on the dance floor as they desperately try to find the beat.
2. Intense, lip-biting facial expression on the faces of all your gay male guests on the dance floor as they mock your straight male guests desperately try to find the beat.

whoopee cushion

Type of novelty gag gift you will be receiving from your husband on your birthday now that you are married and he feels romantic gifts are no longer necessary.

Wiccan

Actual beliefs of the *supposedly* non-denominational person chosen by your spouse to officiate at your wedding, who will go into a fugue state while calling on the horned god, and who will have to be restrained from sacrificing a goat at the altar. (See also *secular officiant*.)

wool socks

One of the items your wife will begin wearing to bed shortly after the wedding. (See also *sweatpants* and *X-Large T-Shirt*.)

WTF

The way your wife signs off on her text messages to you now. (See also *xxx*.)

X

Mark your enraged betrothed will draw through each paragraph of the pre-nuptial agreement that your lawyer dropped on their doorstep two days before the wedding.

X chromosome

Part of human genetic coding responsible for, among other things, the dust ruffle, the pillow sham, pot-pourri, soap operas, and ballroom dancing.

X-large T-shirt

One of the items your wife will begin wearing to bed shortly after the wedding. (See also *sweat-pants* and *wool socks*.)

Xerox

1. Machine at your husband's office upon which, under the influence of several office Christmas party cocktails, he will sit with his pants down in order to create dozens of grainy, but very identifiable, photocopies of his posterior.
2. Machine at your local library upon which your husband will soon be printing several hundred copies of his resume.

xxx

The way your wife used to sign off on her text messages before marriage (See also *WTF.*)

x's and o's

What your football coach father-in-law will draw in permanent marker on a white linen tablecloth while trying to explain to your Seattle Seahawks-loving brother why Pete Carroll's decision to pass on the goal line in Super Bowl XLIX was actually the right call. (See also *deposit.*)

X-Acto knife

Razor blade tool you will use to cut your spouse's wacky little brother out of dozens of wedding photos that he ruined by making "bunny ears" behind your head.

X-ray

What you will drive your husband to the emergency room to receive after you clock him with a twelve-pound ceramic centerpiece after one too many Rudolph the Red-Nosed Reindeer comments. (See also *zit*.)

Y chromosome

Part of human genetic coding responsible for, among other things, the desire to urinate outdoors, the yelling of "Free Bird" at classical piano recitals, the wearing of baseball caps in fine restaurants, and the desire to chew "spit tobacco."

yam

Variety of sweet potato, popular at Thanksgiving, which you are never quite able to prepare the way his mother does.

yawn

1. The involuntary intake of air, frequently due to boredom or fatigue.
2. What you will be doing when the videographer has your face in extreme close-up during the part of the ceremony where your wife tearfully recites to you the heartfelt vows she painstakingly wrote herself.

year

The exact length of time that will pass from the day you get married to the day you forget your first anniversary.

yelling

What your spouse will accuse you of doing during an argument, even though you are only speaking LOUDLY and CLEARLY in an effort to help him or her understand how wrong he or she is.

yes

Wifespeak for "maybe."

YMCA

1. Health club you'll join in a burst of New Year's resolution fitness energy and visit a total of six times in twelve months.
2. Song played by DJ at your wedding that will cause the dance floor to be jammed with people singing along to the lyrics that celebrate the joys of having anonymous, homosexual relations in locker rooms.

YouTube

Website where a suspiciously close-up, hi-def movie of your left breast, popping out of your wedding gown as you dance, will be posted by the time the cake is served. (See also *emerge*.)

yoga

1. Fitness and lifestyle activity your wife will engage in to keep her fit, flexible, and calm.
2. Fitness and lifestyle activity your husband will try and then abandon after finding out how unfit, inflexible, and not-at-all calm he is.

yoga pants

1. Tight, stretchy, almost see-through garment the videographer's sexy assistant will wear at your wedding reception which will be so distracting that the band will botch the father-daughter dance song and all the groomsmen will develop a sudden serious interest in the wedding video business. (See also *underwear*.)
2. Go-to attire thrown on by your wife regardless of occasion, which signifies the exact moment when she gave up on trying to impress you and look put together.

your breath

What you needn't bother holding, while waiting for your husband to hold the door, your chair, your coat or your hand anymore.

Y

zaftig

The Yiddish word you use to describe you best friend's size 22 figure to the dressmaker creating the brides-maid dresses, unaware that she is standing right behind you and is already angry because no one noticed her recent four-pound weight loss. (See also *zero*.)

zebra

The print on the panties your mini-dress-wearing niece has chosen to wear, which becomes quite obvious during the spontaneous limbo contest. (See also *limbo*.)

zero

The chances that your best friend will still be in the wedding after hearing you say this. (See also *zaftig*.)

zillionaire

What the only other guy who ever proposed to you became after you broke his heart and he went on to write the most perfect love song in history. Which your husband will want to dance your first dance to.

zinc

1. Kind of tablets you will obsessively gulp in the weeks before your wedding to ward off any potential illness.
2. The kind of poisoning you will then get, landing you in the emergency room the night before your wedding.

zip

What will be left of your savings after your husband "invests" it with a friend of a friend who knows a guy whose cousin has a "can't miss" stock tip. (See also *nest egg*.)

zirconium

What your "diamond" will turn out to be made out of, thanks to your fiancé's "frugality."

Z

zit

Spectacular facial blemish that will appear on your nose the morning of your nuptials, resulting in your husband making jokes about Rudolph the Red-Nosed Reindeer throughout the reception. (See also *X-ray.*)

ZZ Top

The only style of tribute band that the talent agency has available after your fifteen-piece string orchestra gets stuck in Peoria the night before your big day. (See also *Jesus Just Left Chicago.*)

ZZZs

What your husband will want after sex on your wedding night. (See also *encore.*)

Marriage is an alliance entered into by a man who can't sleep with the window shut, and a woman who can't sleep with the window open.

—George Bernard Shaw